MANDOLIN

BILL MONROE

16 GEMS

AUTHENTIC MANDOLIN TRANSCRIPTIONS

Mandolin transcriptions by Butch Baldassari and Rob Haines
Vocal parts transcribed by Jeff Story

Cover photo: Michael Ochs Archives/Venice, CA

ISBN 0-7935-9573-8

HAL•LEONARD® CORPORATION

7777 W. BLUEMOUND RD. P.O. BOX 13819 MILWAUKEE, WI 53213

Visit Hal Leonard Online at
www.halleonard.com

BILL MONROE
16 GEMS

CONTENTS

P R E F A C E

It is difficult, maybe even impossible, to really capture and transcribe in written music what Bill Monroe's mandolin must have sounded like. Granted, we are hearing them as recorded. However, if we could have heard him live on stage at the Ryman Auditorium in 1945-1949, we might be hard-pressed to notate all that his style and spirit had to say about the music he created and where it came from. Bill's music was not about notes. It was about being high (the vocals) and lonesome, with probably a preference to the blues. Most certainly it was about his style of mandolin playing. Bill used to say that his songs and tunes "really told a story!" For instance, Bill's song "Dream" is about a dream where the sound of the dream is Bill's hound dogs barking from the bottom of a well. Bill Monroe's music was influenced by many things, including the Scotch bagpipe, gospel music, and the black blues of guitarist Arnold Schulz.

Our intent as transcribers of these classic Monroe songs is to paint as accurate a musical picture as possible of the Monroe style of Bluegrass mandolin. With the aid of the original recordings, and the music and tablature, one can embark on an accurate and fascinating study of Bill Monroe's sizable contribution to American music.

Butch Baldassari and Rob Haines

Kentucky Waltz

Words and Music by Bill Monroe

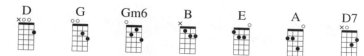

"Kentucky Waltz" was Bill's first vocal tune, written in 1940. This kickoff makes great use of shifting between the first and third positions and always being as melodic as possible. To accompany the vocal, the last two measures end up on a D chord.

𝄋 Verse

(2.) waltz - ing that night in Ken - tuck-y _____ be-neath the beau - ti - ful har - vest
simile on repeat

moon. _____ And I was the boy that was luck-y, _____ but it

Bridge

all end - ed too _____ soon. As I sit here _____ on in the

moon - light _____ I see your smil - ing face. _____ And I

To Coda ⊕

Chorus

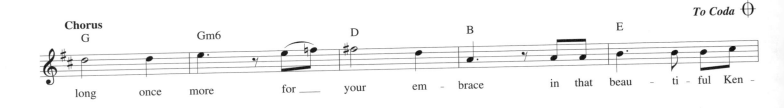

long once more for _____ your em - brace in that beau - ti - ful Ken -

Fiddle Solo   *D.S. al Coda*

tuck - y _____ waltz. _____   2. We were

⊕ *Coda*

tuck - y _____ waltz.

6

True Life Blues

Words and Music by Bill Monroe

This is one of the many classic intros. These licks really define Bill's sound in the key of A. Note the C♮ blues notes in measures 2, 4, 10, 12, and 14. Also the octaves in measures 1, 2, 9, and 10 add lots of power. Memorize this one.

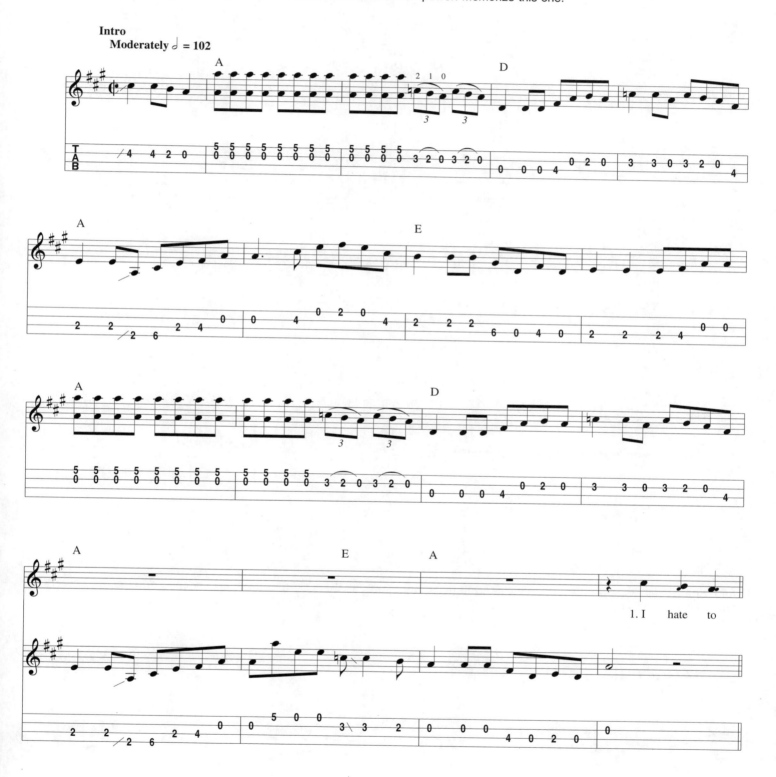

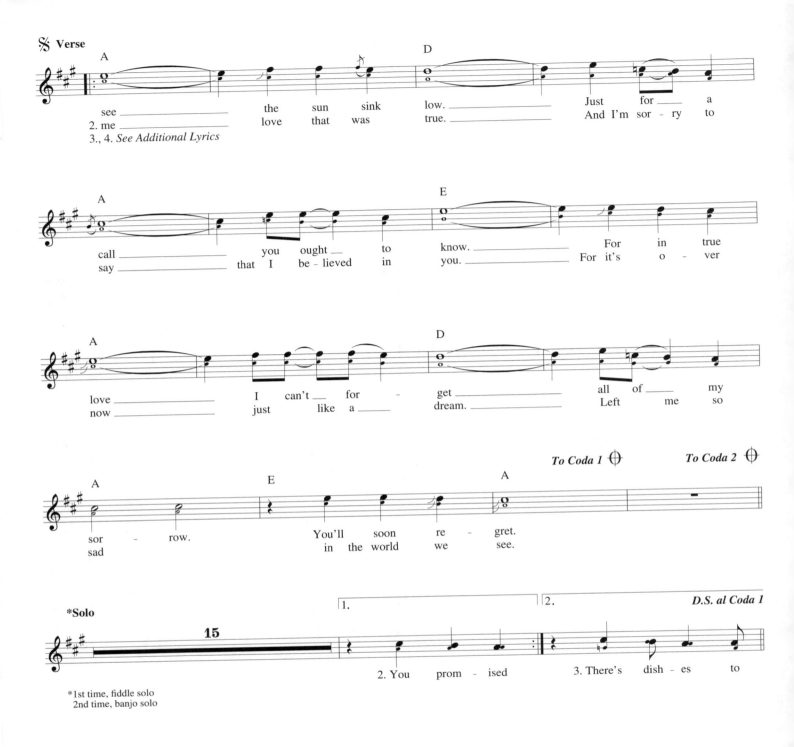

A lot of the melodic and blues ideas included here are the same as the kickoff, but the approach is tremolo, and a very fast and powerful one at that.

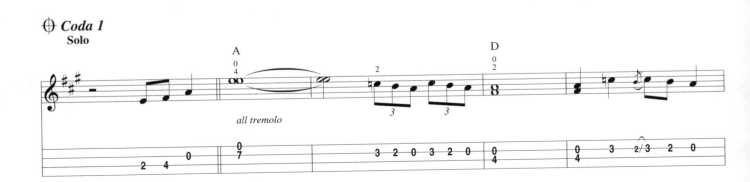

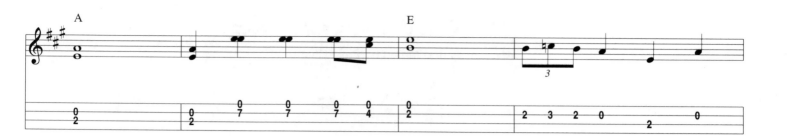

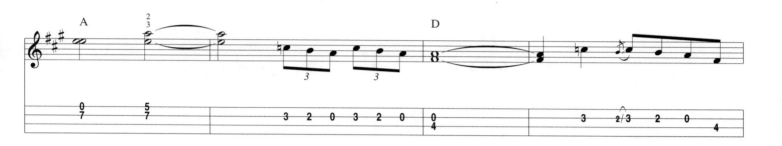

D.S. al Coda 2

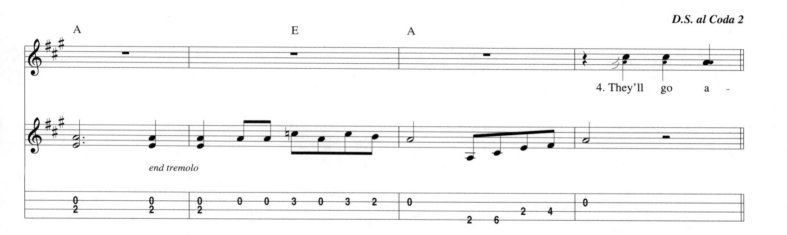

4. They'll go a-

end tremolo

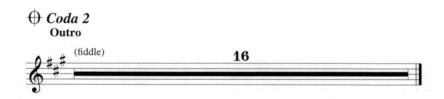

⊕ Coda 2
Outro

(fiddle)

16

Additional Lyrics

3. There's dishes to wash, and a house to clean.
There's washing to do, oh, it seems so mean.
That a million words, I can't explain.
Think of this girl, for I changed her name.

4. They'll go away, and leave you at home.
They never care if you're alone.
They seem to forget they've got a wife.
This story is sad, but it's a true life.

Nobody Loves Me

Words and Music by Zeke Clements

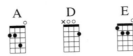

This kickoff alternates between tremolo phrases and downstrokes—common practice with Monroe style. Bill uses this on the kickoff and first solo. The second solo uses syncopation while at the same time being very melodic. Solo B resembles Solo 1, but there are always some subtleties to be studied—that is the beauty of the style.

emp - ty _____ and full ___ of tears. I long for

true love, _____ searched ev - 'ry - where. No - bod - y

To Coda 1
To Coda 2

loves me, no - bod - y cares.

Mandolin Solo

Additional Lyrics

2. Searching for true love has been in vain.
Two years my heart has suffered with pain.
Life's lonesome burden now I must bear.
Nobody loves me, nobody cares.

3. I've sold my pillow, I dream of love.
Through space I gaze at the stars above.
They seem to whisper from way up there,
"Nobody loves me, nobody cares."

Goodbye Old Pal

Words and Music by Bill Monroe

*Mandolin

*Fiddle arr. for mandolin.

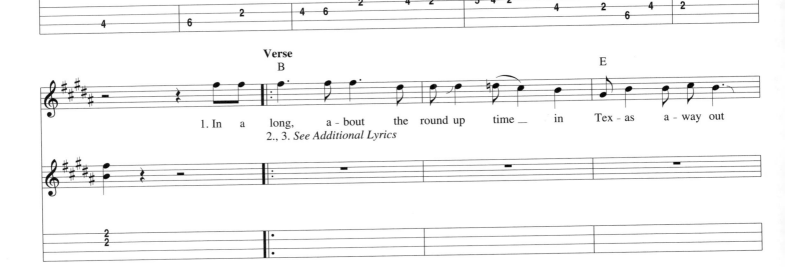

1. In a long, a-bout the round up time __ in Tex-as a-way out
2., 3. *See Additional Lyrics*

Additional Lyrics

2. My best pal was my old main horse.
   Now he's gone to rest.
   I laid him down beneath that mound
   In Texas way out west.
   Where the cactus blooms over his grave
   By when the coyotes cry,
   I know he sleeps in perfect peace
   Beneath the Texas sky.

3. Dear old pal, it breaks my heart
   To leave you here alone.
   Now I go and ride the range
   All on the Texas throne.
   But my love for you, old pal,
   It still lingers on.
   I will always think of you
   Although you're dead and gone.

Blue Grass Special

Words and Music by Bill Monroe

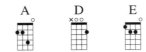

This is another powerful workout in the key of A. It's basically a blues tune. The first pass is the melody. Solo 2 is played out of the A chord position. Almost no open strings are played. Pay attention to the left hand fingerings on the second line and the last two measures. Downstrokes again here—play the blues.

Guitar Solo

Start out with figures that are major chord arpeggios with the F♯ added. It sounds technical but it is a classic Monroe run and is very effective. You go back to first position for this one.

Mandolin Solo

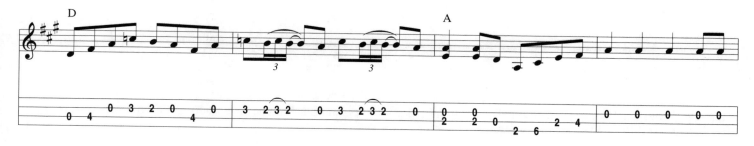

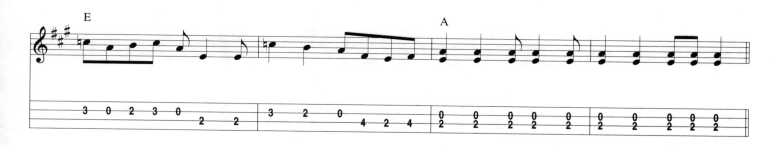

17

Bass Solo

This is a solid tremolo for nine measures, followed by some closed chord licks.

Mandolin Solo

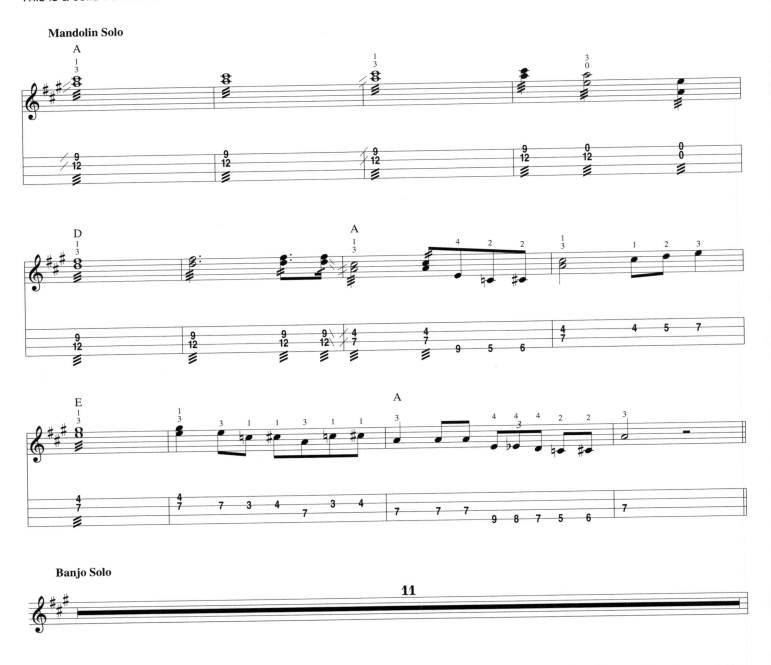

Banjo Solo

This solo again uses blues notes (C♮). The "hammering on and pulling off" technique is used again as well, using repetition and syncopation to make a simple but powerful twelve measures.

Mandolin Solo

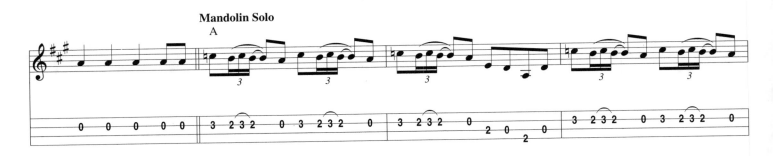

Accordion Solo

Again, this resembles Solo 3. The differences occur when the solo gets to the E chord. Slight changes, but it's still effective.

Mandolin Solo

Heavy Traffic Ahead

Words and Music by Bill Monroe

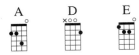

More blues in A—this tune is a closed chord solo. After a few of these in this key, you will start to develop a real *Monroe* vocabulary.

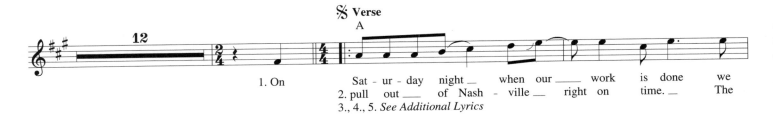

1. On Sat-ur-day night __ when our __ work is done we
2. pull out __ of Nash-ville __ right on time. __ The
3., 4., 5. *See Additional Lyrics*

load our mu-sic up on the run. {Heav-y traf-fic a-head, _____ heav-y
blue grass spec-ial is right on time.}

traf-fic a-head. We got to ram-ble, ram-ble _____

To Coda

_ with heav-y traf-fic a-head.

1., 3., 4.

*Solo

3rd time, D.S. al Coda

2. We

**1st time, banjo solo
2nd time, fiddle solo
3rd time, banjo solo*

2. Solo

3. We

⊕ *Coda*

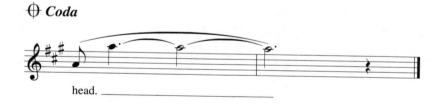

head. _____

Additional Lyrics

3. We traveled around from state to state.
The blue grass boys are never late.
Heavy traffic ahead, heavy traffic ahead.
We got to ramble, ramble with heavy traffic ahead.

4. A later in the evening, about sundown,
You we've conquered some other town.
Heavy traffic ahead, heavy traffic ahead.
We got to ramble, ramble with heavy traffic ahead.

5. We do our work with a good will.
On Friday night we head for next 'ville.
Heavy traffic ahead, heavy traffic ahead.
We got to ramble, ramble with heavy traffic ahead.

Summertime Is Past and Gone

Words and Music by Bill Monroe

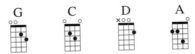

On this tune Bill plays the middle solo between the banjo and fiddle. The solo starts on the IV chord in the second position for four bars. There's lots of great tremolo. Then it goes back to a powerful-sounding open A string and winds up with more great double stops over the D, or V Chord.

⊕ *Coda 1*

Banjo Solo

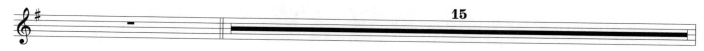

Mandolin Solo

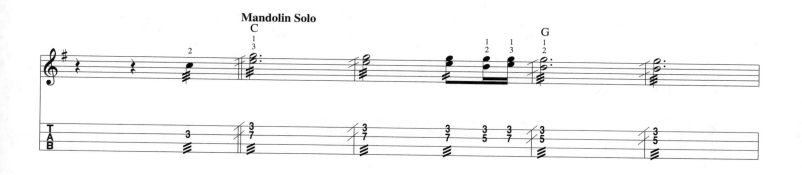

Fiddle Solo

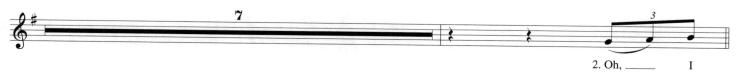

2. Oh, _____ I

Verse

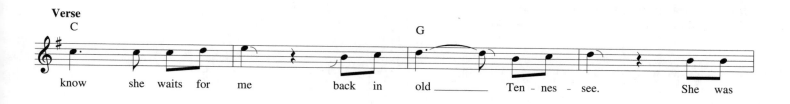

know   she   waits   for   me   back   in   old _____ Ten - nes - see.   She   was

D.S. al Coda 2

sent   to   me   from   God _____ a - bove. _____   Now   the

⊕ *Coda 2*

loved. _____

I'm Going Back to Old Kentucky

Words and Music by Bill Monroe

This is one of the ultimate classic bluegrass mandolin kickoffs. You should really try to memorize this one and try to play it as fast as possible. It looks easy, but it's really about speed and power. Bill's second solo is almost identical to his intro solo.

Additional Lyrics

2. Linda Lu, she is a beauty;
   Both pretty brown eyes and love so well.
   I'm a-going back to old Kentucky;
   Nevermore to sing farewell.

3. Linda Lu, you know I love you.
   I long for you each night and day.
   When the roses bloom in old Kentucky
   I'll be coming back to stay.

It's Mighty Dark to Travel

Words and Music by Bill Monroe

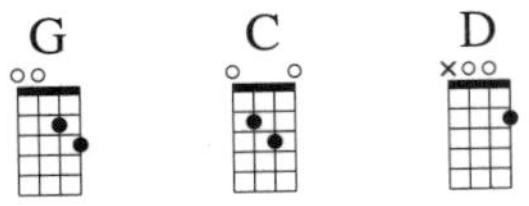

Here are some great ideas for the key of G. Note measure 7 where Bill uses an open D with the B below for the G chord sound. Bill's solo after the second chorus is similar to his solo on the intro.

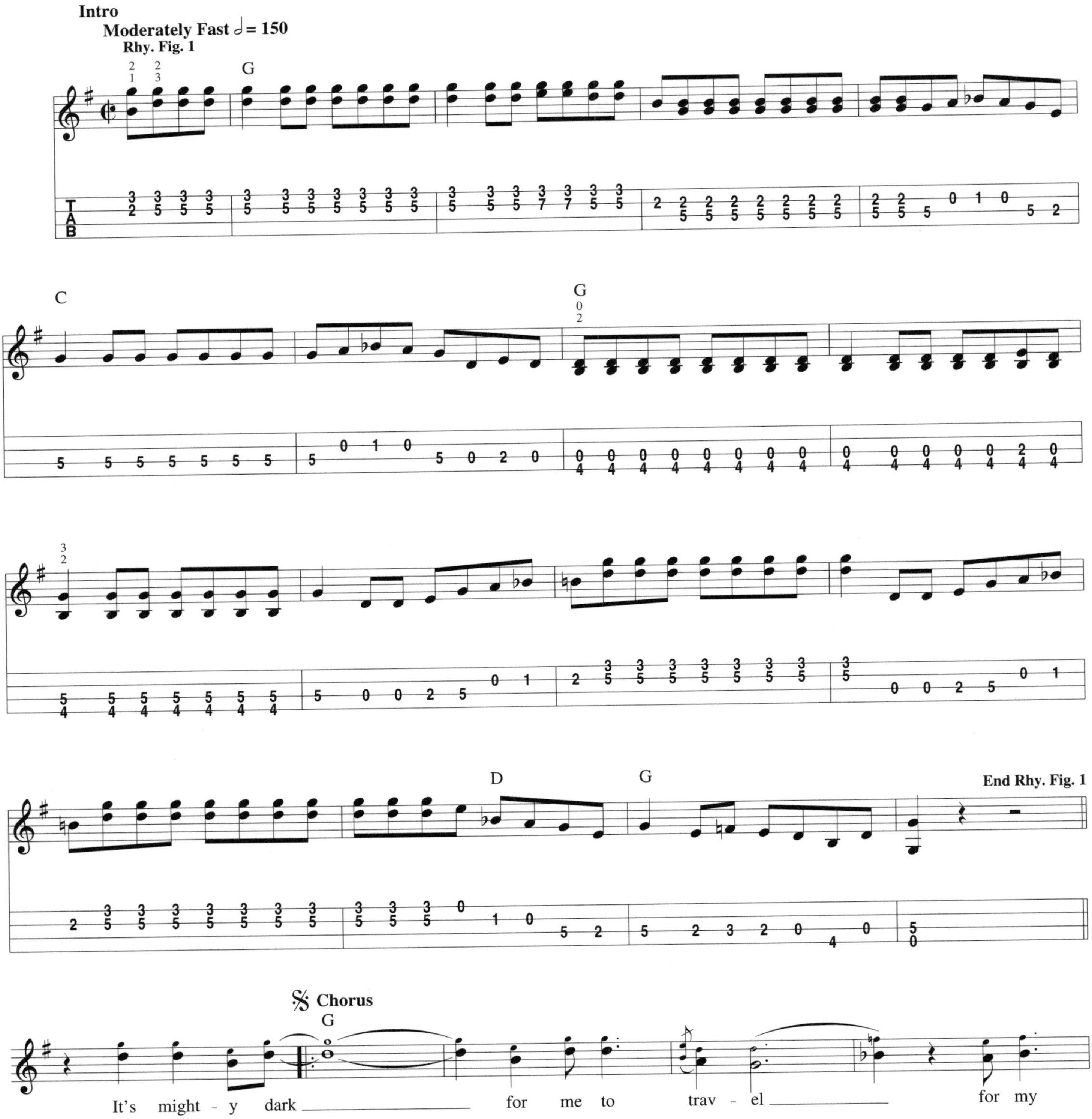

Copyright © 1950 by Unichappell Music Inc.
Copyright Renewed
International Copyright Secured All Rights Reserved

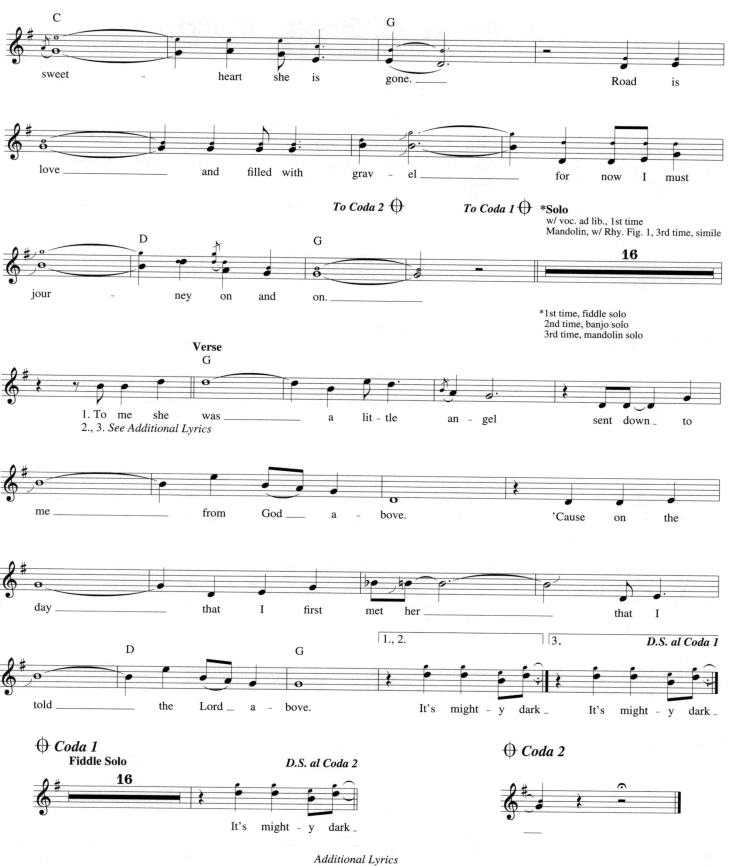

Additional Lyrics

2. Many a night we strolled together
   Talking love I know so fair.
   My love for her will never vanish
   For I know I need her there.

3. Traveling down this lonesome highway
   Thinking how my love is gold.
   Knowing soon we'll be together;
   She's the only love I've known.

Blue Grass Breakdown

Music by Bill Monroe

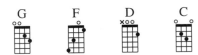

This tune, along with "White House Blues" and "Rawhide," are probably some of the most important pieces in the Monroe repertoire. In addition to demanding tremendous speed from the player, knowledge of double stops and position playing all come into play to create one of the classic bluegrass instrumentals. If we just look at the music or tablature, this tune doesn't look to hard. However, putting all of the notes together at Bill's blazing tempo might take some effort. If you can master this one you will own the key of G.

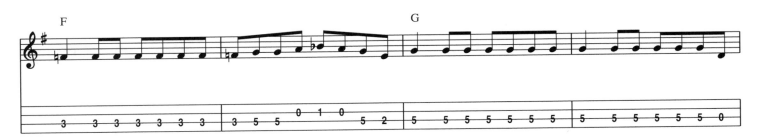

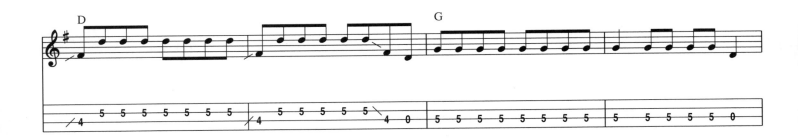

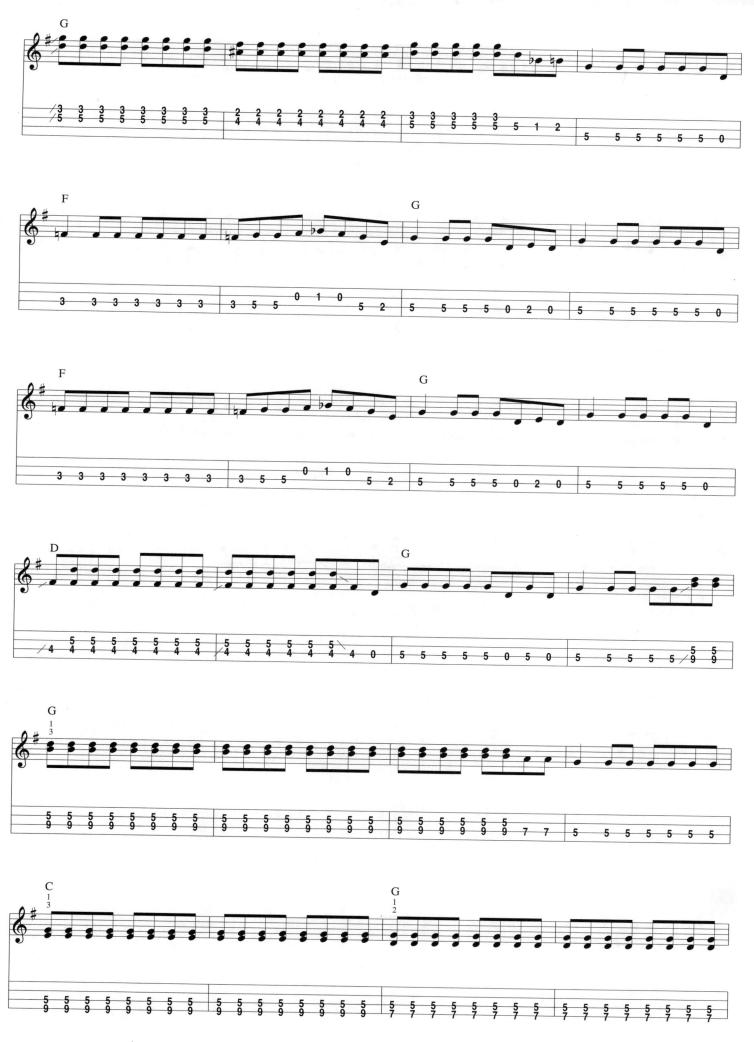

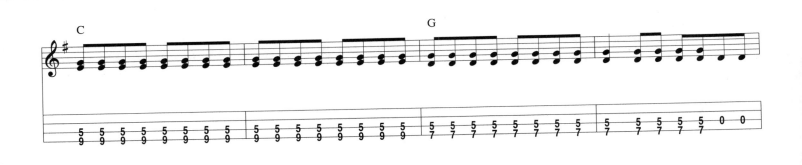

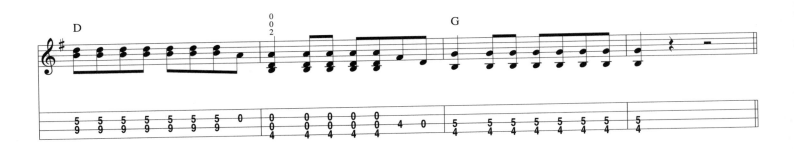

Banjo Solo

Mandolin Solo

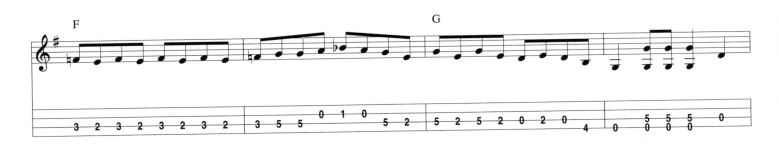

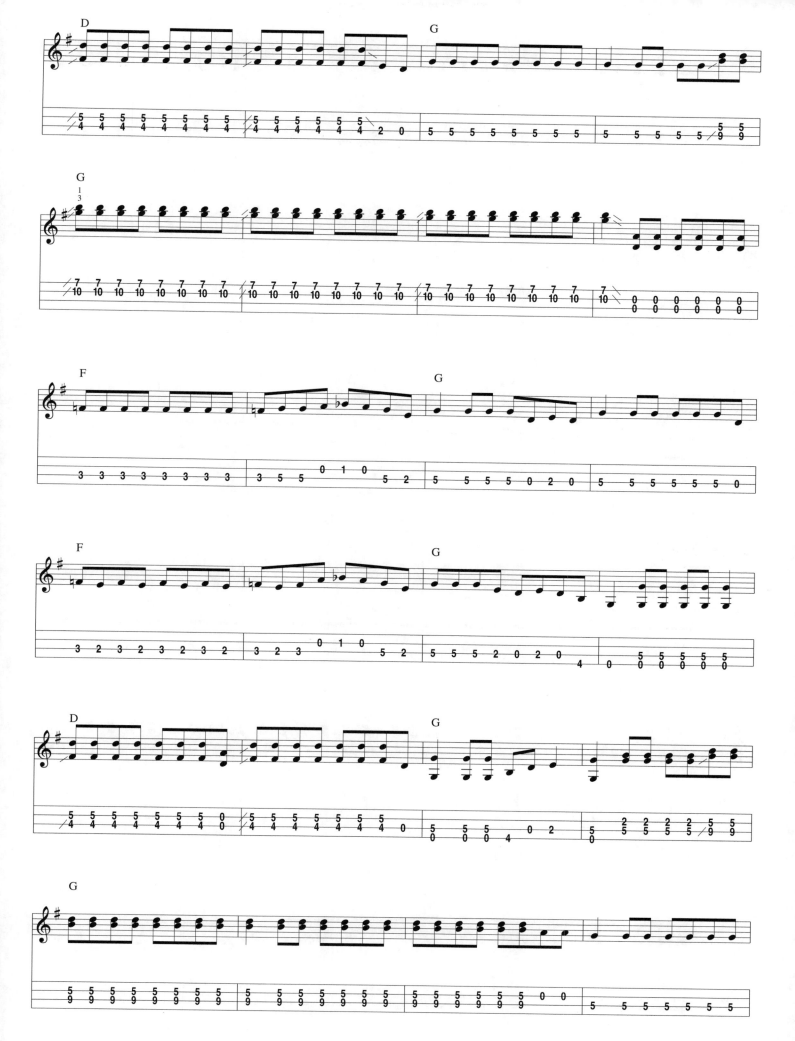

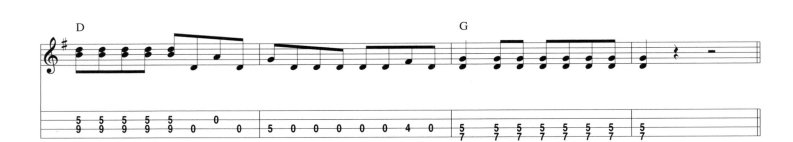

Fiddle Solo

Solo

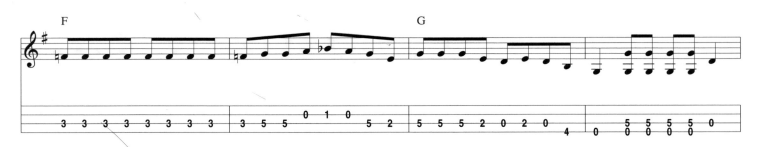

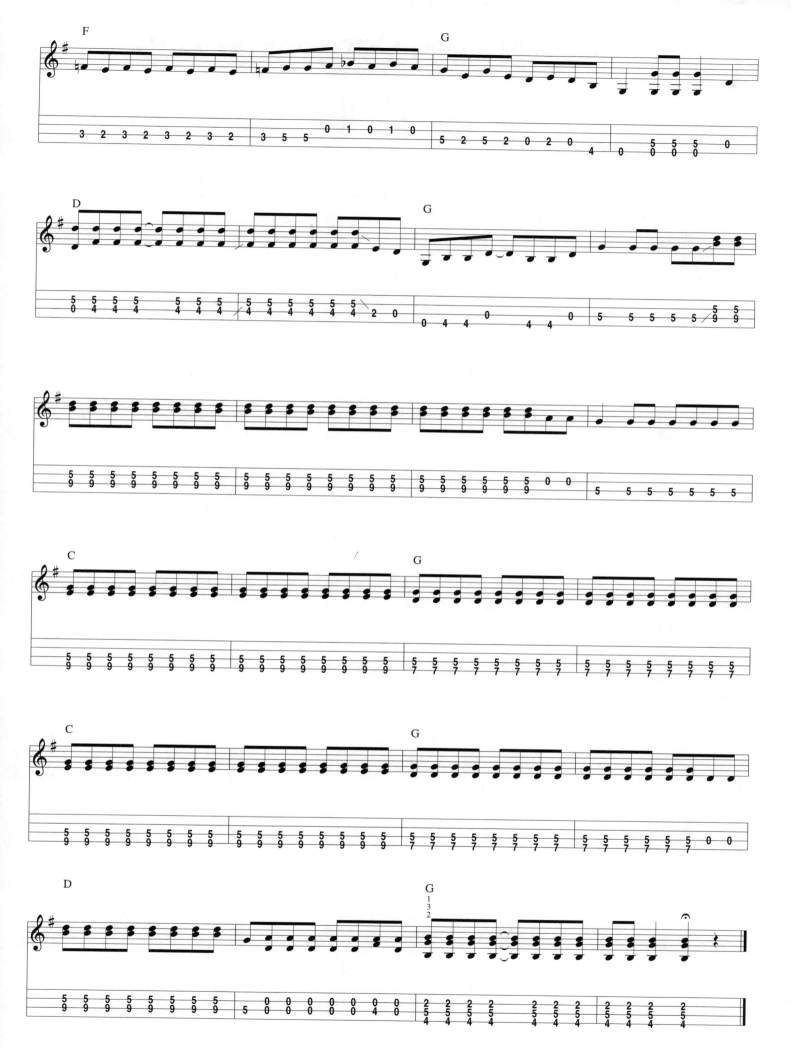

Sweetheart You Done Me Wrong

Words and Music by Bill Monroe and Lester Flatt

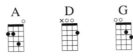

This kickoff starts right out of a D chord, then into an A chord, and then right back to the D. The melody is lick-oriented, but really works. Then Bill's solo is a half verse played out of the D chord position using some nice double stops and tremolo. The solo ends with the motives stated in the kickoff.

Old Crossroad Is Waitin'

Words and Music by Bill Monroe

This tune uses a classic kickoff in the key of G. It uses blues notes right over the D chord and ends with a guitar run. We have also included a backup lick that Bill seemed to use a lot in this tune. Try playing it in other keys. Bill plays the intro solo at the end of each chorus.

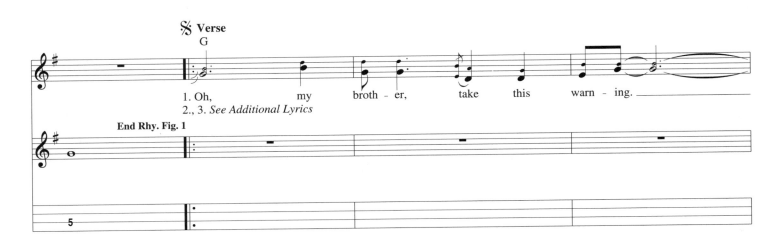

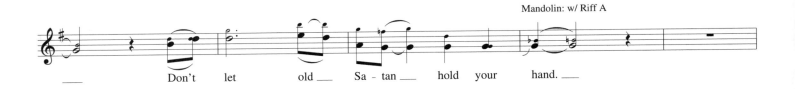

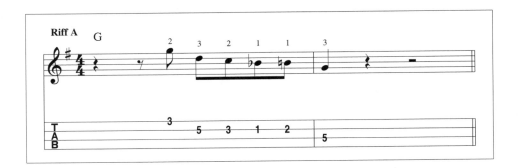

You'd be lost in sin for - ev - er. _____ You'd

Mandolin: w/ Riff A

nev - er _____ reach _____ the prom - ised land. The

Chorus
G

old cross _____ road _____ now is wait - ing. _____ Which

one are _____ you _____ go - ing to take? _____ One leads

To Coda ⊕

down to de - struc - tion, _____ the oth - er to the pearl - y

| 1., 2.

Mandolin: w/ Rhy. Fig. 1, simile

2nd time, D.S. al Coda

G   D   G

gates.

⊕ *Coda*

rit.

to _____ the pearl - y gates.

Additional Lyrics

2. One road leads up to Heaven
The other goes down below.
Jesus, our savior, will protect you.
He'll guide you by the old crossroad.

3. Soon your life will be over.
You'll have to face the old crossroad.
Will you be ready then, my brother,
To shun the one goes down below?

Remember the Cross

Words and Music by Bill Monroe and Howard Watts

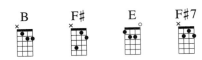

This tune uses a simple but effective traditional gospel kickoff. Try moving to other keys and see how it works. The first solo is *high lonesome* and the second one bluesy. Both solos are solid powerful statements from the Bluegrass Quartet's instrumentalist.

foot - steps each day. ____ He shed His blood for you and He

shed His blood for me. Nev - er cast that cross ____ a - side.

Mandolin Solo
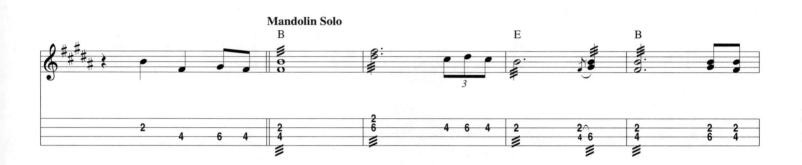

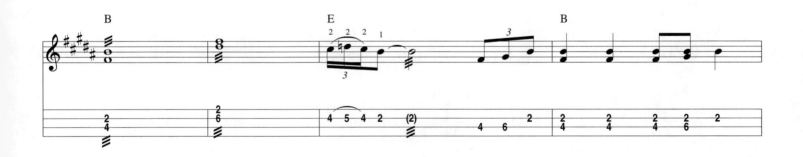

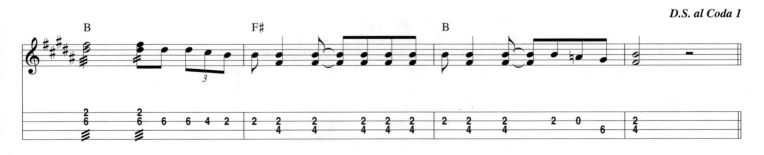

⊕ *Coda 1*

Mandolin Solo

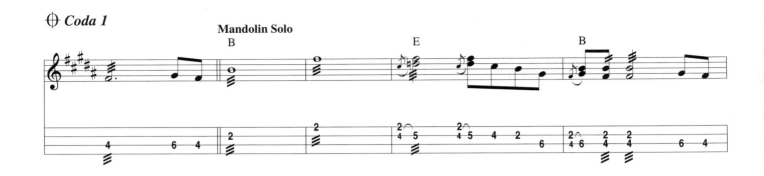

D.S. al Coda 2

⊕ *Coda 2*

cross _____ a - side.

Additional Lyrics

2. Never let other people lead you astray.
   Teach His words to them if you can.
   They must think of the cross on which Jesus died
   And get ready to meet Him someday.

3. When Jesus comes down from Heaven above
   And you haven't thought of that cross,
   He'll cast you aside in the twinkling of an eye
   And you won't see His blessed home of love.

Shine Hallelujah Shine

Words and Music by Bill Monroe

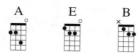

Another simple kickoff but it really gets the job done. The two solos are very similar—the second solo uses drones and stylistic double stops. This type of solo can get you a lot of mileage in the key of A.

Additional Lyrics

2. Jesus, the Lord, is now my refuge.
   Daily He leads me by the hand.
   He will be my steady comfort
   'Til I reach the glory land.
   So press along with hopes eternal
   Springing in this heart of mine.
   When I enter the gates of Heaven
   I will shine, shine, shine.

3. We were burdened with many affliction,
   Often unsightly things we did.
   But we'll all be like our Savior
   When we reach that home up there.
   Daily I walk in His dear footsteps
   Growing more like Him all the time.
   When I enter the gates of Heaven
   I will shine, shine, shine.

Can't You Hear Me Calling

Words and Music by Bill Monroe

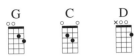

More great stuff for the key of G, consisting mostly of melody. There are some bluesy phrases in measures 6 and 11 where syncopation and licks get you to the end. Listen and learn!

Additional Lyrics

2. I remember now the night we parted.
   A big mistake has caused it all.
   If you'll return sunshine will follow.
   To stay away would be my fall.

3. The days are dark, my little darling.
   Oh, how I need your sweet embrace.
   When I awoke the sun was shining.
   When I looked up I saw your face.

Travelin' This Lonesome Road

Words and Music by Bill Monroe

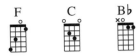

A great solo in F, second position—pay attention to left hand fingerings to keep you in position. Try and capture the use of double stops and open strings in measures 6 and 7. Then there is some fierce tremolo in measures 10, 11, and 12. Memorize this and you will have learned the key of F.

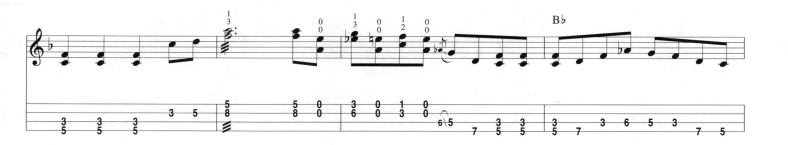

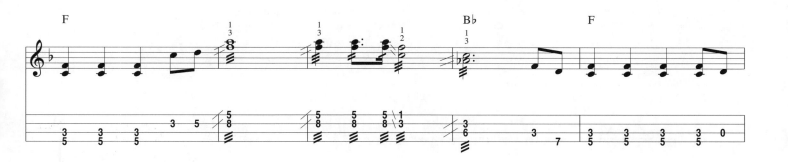

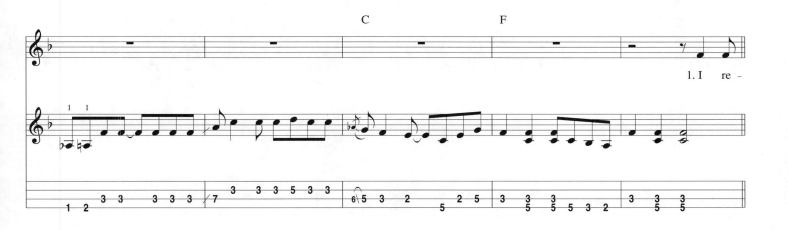

Verse

mem – ber dear __ not long a – go __ you said you'd be __ my __ own. _____ I
2. All I do __ is roam a – round __ and look for you __ my __ dear. _____ I

nev – er thought __ you'd go a – way __ and leave me all __ a – lone. _____ The
know I searched __ ten thou – sand miles. __ Oh, how I need __ you near. _____ You

kind of love ___ you had for me ___ I find, sweet - heart, ___ grows cold. But
broke my heart ___ you left me here. ___ Now I'm grow - ing old. Why

To Coda 2 ⊕   *D.S. al Coda 1*

now you're gone ___ and left me here ___ to trav - el this lone - some road. ___ } I'm
did you ___ go ___ and leave me dear ___ to trav - el this lone - some road? ___ }

⊕ *Coda 1*
Fiddle Solo   *D.S.S. al Coda 2*

19

⊕ *Coda 2*

Chorus

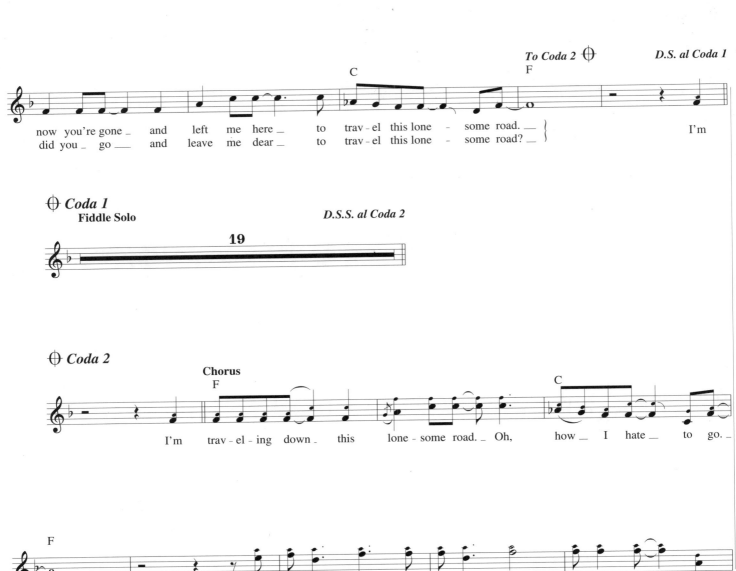

I'm trav - el - ing down ___ this lone - some road. ___ Oh, how ___ I hate ___ to go. ___

The wind and storm are rag - ing high and it's aw - ful

cold. _____ My mind gets back to you, sweet - heart, and I love ___ you

so. _____ Now you've gone ___ and left me here ___ to trav - el this lone - some road.